TESTIMONIALS

A very practical guide to finding, writing, and fulfilling your God given purpose, mission, and vision. Williams takes you step by step through, what is an otherwise challenging process and makes it easy.

~KM

This was an amazing read! The plan of action was easy to follow and implement into my lifestyle. I especially enjoyed reading the "Life Questions" section because it helped me to really figure out who I am and what mark I want to leave on this earth while I'm here. I'm so glad Coach Brian Williams challenges his readers to think differently!

~Queayna Battle

DIRECTIONS FOR LIFE:

Develop and Live Your Purpose, Mission, Vision, and Plan

COACH BRIAN WILLIAMS

Edited by MARTHA BOOTLE
Edited by LISA LUKE EASTERLING
Edited by KATHY SWIGLE

COPYRIGHT

Direction For Life: Develop and live your Purpose, Mission, Vision, and Plan

By Coach Brian Williams

Copyright © Brian Williams 2013 All rights reserved. No part of this book may be reproduced, stored in a retrieval system, or transmitted in any form, without the written permission of Brian Williams (you can reach me at www.coachbrianwilliams@gmail.com).

Published by: Inspired for Life Media, California

Scriptures used are from the New International Version® and are noted as in NIV in the document., NIV®. Copyright ©1973, 1978, 1984, 2011 by Biblica, Inc. TM Used by permission of Zondervan. All rights reserved worldwide. www.zondervan.com. The "NIV" and "New International Version" are trademarks registered in the United States Patent and Trademark Office by Biblica, Inc.TM.

Edited by Martha Bootle, Lisa Luke Easterling, and Kathy Swigle

❦ Created with Vellum

CONTENTS

Introduction	vii
More Books and Resources by Coach Brian Williams	1
About the Author	5
Do You Know Jesus?	6
Acknowledgments	11
How to Use this Book	13
Life Questions	15
Developing Your Personal Purpose Statement	17
Developing Your Personal Mission Statement	28
Developing Your Personal Vision Statement	35
Plan of Action: How to Live Your Purpose, Mission, and Vision	46
Live the Adventure	54

INTRODUCTION

There is a purpose and plan for each and every one of us each day of our lives that we are on this earth. Unfortunately, most people not only are off track in living it, they don't even know what it is. As Zig Ziglar said, many people have become a "Wandering Generality instead of a Meaningful Specific."

A little over 20 years ago, I was off track. Although I grew up in church and was a "Christian", I was miserable in life. I was not living the way I should have been and didn't even know what path to take. Over time, God transformed me and showed me His purpose for me and my mission while on this earth. He also helped me put in place the ways to manage time, set my direction (goals) based on His plan, and to succeed His way.

Before you can know if you are on God's path in your daily walk, it's important to start with a bigger picture. You need to know and commit to the purpose God has for you. This is your "mission" to achieve while here on earth by following the dreams and visions God has put in your heart.

Once you have written these out and you are confident in God's commitment to you, and your commitment to Him, you can fulfill His plan for your life. This is done through praying, planning, organizing, and managing what you need as you follow Him each step along the path. It is team work with God. He won't just move everything on your behalf while you sit around watching TV. While He doesn't expect you to be successful on your own, He will open the doors as you walk with Him.

Directions for Life was written to help you discover God's purpose for your life and to help you know your mission so you can achieve it as you walk with Him. It will help you get excited about the vision God gives you and then help you take practical steps to getting it done as you walk by faith. This book is simple and easy to follow, but can be life-changing.

MORE BOOKS AND RESOURCES BY COACH BRIAN WILLIAMS

Thank you for purchasing this book and deciding to take action to talk (God's) truth to yourself! God will bless you for it.

Please write a quick review of this book on Amazon.com to help get the word out to others who are looking for a Biblical tool to change their own lives.

If you are looking to grow closer to God, and fulfill the purpose He has for you, Coach Brian Williams has also developed additional books, tools, and resources to assist you. God bless you as you follow Christ.

Am I Saved?

Many Christians walk through life uncertain of their salvation, associating being saved with their own efforts rather than seeing it as a gift of God's grace. This book provides a solid answer to this vital question.

Made to Change the World: Your Life Matters

This book will encourage you to know God's calling, then provide the tools to live it in every area of your life with an impact that will change the world around you.

Made to Change the World: Your Life Matters Small Group Study

This eight-week study not only walks your group through how to understand God's calling, but also provides the way to change and live it out.

Lifewise: How to Live by God's Wisdom

Grow closer to God through this helpful resource that will challenge you to not only think deeper in your faith, but to make the changes in your life in order to walk closer with God each day.

Talk Truth to Yourself

We easily get off track in life because we believe things that are not true about God and His promises. This book will teach you how to know and live the truth to receive God's promises.

Life Balance for Christians - It's Not What You Think

Balanced living in God's eyes isn't the same as what the world considers balance. More important than us figuring out how to balance our own lives is surrendering each area to God. This book also contains a six-week study guide that will help you evaluate and assess your life balance as you submit all the areas of your life to God. You will set goals and make progress as God leads.

Theology of Behavior Change: How to Make Lasting Change

Many Christians want to change areas in their life or follow God more closely in faith, but do not know how to make changes that last. This book explains how to change and gives supporting tools.

Walk With God Today: Daily Christian Devotional

This devotional provides daily reading sections and action steps for spiritual growth. Best seller on Kindle and over 9,000 copies have been downloaded so far.

For all of these books, as well as additional resources to help you fully live the life God desires for you and impact the world around you, go to www.madetochangetheworld.com. Make sure to watch the short video on our home page and to register to get free weekly emails with videos, tools, and encouragement to support you in your walk with God.

Pastors and Ministry Leaders – See the "Pastors and Ministry Leaders" tab at our website www.madetochangetheworld.com for tools to help you disciple those you lead.

ABOUT THE AUTHOR

Brian Williams is a double Board-Certified Coach and a Professional Certified Coach (PCC) through the International Coaching Federation. He has coached thousands of people and has led a staff of coaches whose combined efforts have positively impacted the lives of many.

Brian has extensive experience in helping people improve key areas of their lives including wellness, career, business, relationships, and most importantly, walking with Jesus. He has helped them fulfill their God-ordained purpose through the direction of Jesus Christ. He partners with each person to help him or her clearly move forward by taking the right steps, and, through accountability and encouragement, to achieve those goals.

Brian is also an ordained pastor through the Anchor Bay Evangelistic Association. He uses his spiritual background and training to help others grow through coaching, and has helped lead prayer ministries, facilitate small groups, and organize various spiritual campaigns and church projects. Brian, along with his wife Claudia and their daughter Ellie, attend and serve at FishHawk Fellowship Church in Lithia, Florida.

DO YOU KNOW JESUS?

This book will be a great help for your walk with Jesus. However, I realize some of you reading this may not know what it means to be a Christian or even if you are one. This section is for you and will help you not only understand what being a Christian means but also help you make the most important decision in your life if you are ready.

I will start with my background and how I became a Christian. In my early 20's, I graduated from college and moved to Florida. Even though I was already becoming successful at a young age, I found myself on Clearwater Beach one Saturday in a miserable state of mind. Even though I had grown up going to church, I ended up hopeless and all the accomplishments, friends, church sermons, and other things I had experienced in life did not bring fulfillment. I asked myself what the purpose was in continuing to move forward in life.

When I got to my lowest low and sat on the beach that day, I looked around at the sky, the ocean, and the birds flying and realized that no man made what I saw and no man controls it. I knew I couldn't make it on my own and needed a bigger purpose and reason for life. I also knew what it meant to turn my life over to God, so I prayed to Jesus and surrendered my life to Him. I knew that I had sinned (missed the mark) many times in my life and asked Jesus to forgive me. I asked Jesus to give me His purpose and direction. I committed to pray and read the Bible every day and promised God that if He would help me out of my miserable mess, I would tell everyone I could about His love and forgiveness and about the transformation in my life. So here I am, writing this to you because of this complete transformation of my life.

I have kept that commitment to spend daily time with Him each morning over the past 20 years. I can probably count on one hand the number of times I have missed praying and Bible reading. There were some big changes God walked me through over the months and years that followed my day at the beach, including putting away my selfish desires, changing my focus, and realigning my thinking in order to believe what is true based on what He says in the Bible. He empowers me to pursue a much bigger and more important purpose for my life here on earth and for eternity.

I have talked with many people and it is easy to see that what the Bible says is true – we all are in the same boat of having sinned in our lives. Sin is the opposite of God's will and is mainly formed from our selfish desires and attitudes. Sin includes things like anger, jealousy, bitterness, fear, unbelieving, immoral thoughts, sexuality outside of marriage, lying, wanting someone else's property, and lust, just to name a few. It is putting yourself and "things" in life as the most important in the place of God. Sin is disobedience to God and not living the way he wants us to live, which is to work together here on this earth through His love.

God not only has a plan for you here on earth, but also for eternity. The problem is that sin separates us from God and causes a chasm between us. This is a chasm we cannot cross on our own because we are the ones who caused it. You may know that in the Old Testament of the Bible, God required people to sacrifice animals to redeem their sins and bridge that chasm. That may sound harsh, but sin is so serious to God that its penalty is death. The payment for sin requires either our own personal death or the death of a substitute.

The great news is that a couple thousand years ago, God made a cataclysmic change by redeeming our sins and removing the separation from Him. He Himself, in the form of His Son, Jesus, came to earth as a baby through a virgin named Mary. This is the real reason we celebrate Christmas. The story doesn't end there, however.

After Jesus was born, He walked the earth and was the only person to live a sinless life and follow God's purpose in every way. At 33 years old, Jesus was put to death. For more details of the amazing life and events of Jesus' life, you can read the books of Matthew, Mark, Luke, and John in the Bible.

Because of Jesus' life and death on the cross, He became the ultimate sacrifice and redemption for our sin. The most exciting part is three days later Jesus rose from the dead and was seen by hundreds of witnesses who not only saw Him, but also talked with Him and even touched his wounds. Jesus did not just die, as have many other religious leaders who are still dead. He rose again and is alive today calling you to Him.

Jesus gave us a way to be forgiven through His sinless blood shed on a cross: He died in our place. You may be familiar with John 3:16, which says, "For God so loved the world that He gave His only son so that whoever believes in Him will not perish but will have eternal life." Another verse in Romans 10 says, "If you declare with your mouth, 'Jesus is Lord', and believe in your heart that God raised him from the dead, you will be saved. For it is with your heart that you believe and are justified, and it is with your mouth that you profess your faith and are saved."

This means that the most incredible thing God could ever do for you, He already did. This means that you don't have to try to face life on your own anymore, but that you will be given a purpose and peace that you can never get anywhere else. It means that you want Him to lead and guide your life. It also means you want to (and will) be with Him for eternity once you leave this earth. In order to bridge that chasm and have a relationship with your heavenly Father, all you have to do is believe. Believe that He died on the cross for you and ask Him to forgive your sins, which again are all the past things you have done wrong in your life. When you ask Him to come into your heart, He will, and He will change your life forever.

If you are ready to turn things over to God and live a full and adventurous life filled with peace and tremendous purpose for now and eternity, here is a prayer for you to pray out loud or in your heart.

"Jesus, I believe you are the son of God and that you died for my sins, then rose again. Thank you for loving me so much that you sacrificed your very life. I know that I have done things in my life that were against your will and purpose. Please forgive me. I want to start new with you! I ask you to come into my life and lead me. I want you to show me your way and the true purpose that you put me on this earth. Thank you, Lord Jesus. I dedicate my life to you. Amen."

Congratulations!

You probably didn't have fireworks go off or hear a voice come down from heaven. You may not have felt anything inside, either, but rest assured that God heard you and He is faithful. What you will probably notice right away, but certainly over time, is a peace inside your heart. You are now part of the family of God, which is a huge family of other believers you will be with for eternity.

It is important to share with someone the decision you made today. You can share it with family or friends. If you have another Christian in your life, I'm sure he or she would love to hear about your decision and so would I. Please email me at hello@madetochangetheworld.com.

A next great step for you would be to attend a local church and/or Bible study group. Make sure the place you attend is using only the Holy Bible as their source of truth and training. Another book to help you more clearly understand salvation and next steps is free for you at my website or on Amazon. It is titled *Am I Saved?* Get your copy by clicking on the Resource tab at www.madetochangetheworld.com.

Now, you may have read all of this and not feel ready to make this change or commitment. I want you to know that God loves you more than you can comprehend! He is faithful and will keep tugging at your heart! If you have questions or need help sorting this out, please email me at hello@madetochangetheworld.com. You may also find great answers and insight by reading the book listed above or *The Case for Christ* by Lee Strobel.

God bless you! Remember that Jesus loves you so much that He died for you.

ACKNOWLEDGMENTS

If you have read any of my testimony above, you will quickly see I would not even be alive today if Jesus Christ hadn't saved and changed me. Without Christ's perfect will and plan, I would not be here to write a book about how He has impacted my life. Thank you, Lord, for saving me through your mercy and grace on the beach that day, and for daily leading me along your path through your Holy Spirit.

I am also thankful to God for Zig Ziglar. Although he wasn't specifically mentioned in my testimony above, God used him as a mentor in my life to help me make changes and follow Christ. Although Zig passed away near the end of 2012, his books, audios, and teachings still impact my life. Each day, I still use the *Zig Ziglar Personal Planner* to plan and organize my day and life. Although my time with Zig was limited, his books and teachings still have an influence on me today.

During the time of my life that I met Zig I was working for a Life and Executive Coaching division of a seminar company and worked closely with a co-worker named Josh Wright who always challenged me about my thoughts in the areas of purpose, mission, and vision. I thank God for his life and appreciate his challenging questions, promptings, and support from my Christian brother. These times of discussion still cause me to pray through and refine areas of my life's direction to make sure they glorify God.

Last, but certainly not least, I am daily thankful to God for my other half – Claudia Williams. Proverbs 18:22 says, "He who finds a wife finds what is good and receives favor from the Lord." I have certainly found great favor from God because I am blessed beyond measure with such a loving, caring, and supportive wife.

There are many others I would like to thank and acknowledge by name, but that would turn this into an encyclopedia instead of one book! So I say from the bottom of my heart to my family and many friends who have supported me, encouraged me, and given me feedback over the years – Thank You! I cannot tell you how much your lives and encouragement mean to me.

HOW TO USE THIS BOOK

This Personal Development book is designed to help you understand the importance of having a purpose, mission, vision, and a powerful plan for your life. It is written from a Christian perspective by applying scripture, promises. and prayer to the formulation of these important areas. I encourage you to pray as you read this so you will have direction from Christ. I also encourage you to journal and put into words what He places on your heart.

This book will help you focus on each section as I describe these key areas, discuss why they are important, show you how to write out your own statements, and help you make sure they are correct for you after you draft them. Once you draft the broader statement you will be able to put a plan in place to establish your best direction and focus for your future. As the saying goes, "A plan well written is already half accomplished."

Reading through this book could take anywhere from several hours to several weeks based on how well you know yourself, the dreams God has given you, and the detail needed in the goals as part of your plan. Don't rush the process! It's also good to get others' feedback and viewpoint. However, if you feel you have answered these questions as led by God, don't let others sway you just because they think differently. Your purpose, mission, and vision statements are uniquely yours as designed by your Heavenly Father.

As always, there is additional support to help you grow. If you find you would like to work with me or another Christian coach to help you draft, implement, and live out these powerful focuses for your life, you can go madetochangetheworld.com or e-mail me at coachbrianwilliams@gmail.com.

In getting started, there are some powerful questions that can get you thinking about your life, your desires, and your future. As you answer these, you will be able to answer the questions that come up in the Purpose and Mission Statement areas.

LIFE QUESTIONS

The following questions can be powerful in your life now, but also for designing your future. Take as much time and space as you need to answer them so you are confident that you have answered them fully.

Four questions from Billy Graham to consider:

1) Who am I?

2) Where do I come from?

3) Where am I headed?

4) What is the purpose for life?

Life Questions:

1) Why are you here on earth?

2) Why is tomorrow worth looking forward to?

3) Why is life important?

4) If you were to die today, how would you like to be remembered?

5) If you were to die today, where would you go for eternity?

Questions about you:

1) Is there anything you would stand up for in a large crowd of people, no matter who disagreed?

2) What do you believe you were designed by God to become?

3) What is your passion for life based upon?

4) What do you want most in life?

5) What is the purpose for doing the things that you do right now?

Questions about God's desire for your life:

1) What are we called to be (as children of God)?

2) Do you consider yourself righteous and holy?

Consider Jeremiah 5:1. "Go up and down the streets of Jerusalem, look around and consider, search through her squares. If you can find but one person who deals honestly and seeks the truth, I will forgive this city."

Could you be that one who could save the city?

DEVELOPING YOUR PERSONAL PURPOSE STATEMENT

What is a purpose statement? Simply put, when we talk about the purpose of our lives, it's our reason for being, summarized in one statement. This sounds easy to develop, but really takes some time, thought, and effort to develop successfully.

There are many worldly books, trainings, and methods for how to draft your own Purpose Statement based solely on who you think you are and all the things you want in this life. The problem is that it is based on "worldly thinking" and, many times, even New Age principles. God wants us to know his purpose for our life and He reveals it as we seek Him. Often in scripture, God asks one of His children to write down something He reveals to them so they don't forget it and can share it with others as needed. Some examples of this in God's Word about the importance of writing things down are:

Habakkuk 2:2 "Then the Lord replied: 'Write down the revelation and make it plain on tablets.'"

Ezekiel 43:11 "Write these down before them so that they may be faithful to its design and follow all its regulations."

Philippians 3:1 "It is no trouble for me to write the same things to you again, and it is a safeguard for you."

A strong purpose statement should come from God's truth, your faith, and your heart. When fully drafted, it will energize and excite you about why you exist and where your life is headed for God's purpose. If you are a Christian, your purpose will be based on God's values—which are His priorities for your life—and through them the Holy Spirit will "ignite" your spirit. If your purpose statement is not based on this core fundamental, then it is probably not really who you are, nor who God created you to be.

Your purpose statement should explain in ONE SENTENCE who you are and why you exist. It should be simple, easy to remember, and easy for anyone to understand. When you consider all the areas of life—spiritual, mental, health, physical, relationships, finances, career, and recreation—they should all fall under this one key purpose statement: your dedication to God. This is the core of why you exist. Everything you do, including your dreams and goals, will relate to your true purpose in life. Keep in mind that the purpose statement does not actually say *how* you will fulfill the purpose or the *result* of the purpose, as those will come later when you draft your personal mission and vision statements.

Why is it important to know your purpose in life? Because without it, you become what Zig Ziglar referred to as a "wandering generality" as opposed to a "meaningful specific".

Research shows that the number one deadly fear for people in modern times is "having lived a meaningless life." That is a powerful statement. This reflects that a lot of people don't fully know why they are on this earth, nor are they living with purpose. Surprisingly, this is even true for Christians. Reading recent Gallop and other polls, many people who say they are Christians don't even know if they believe the Bible is true or understand their actual purpose on earth. This is a sad fact that holds people back from fulfilling God's plan for their life.

It actually is the sign of a bigger problem within this generation that is causing world issues and rebellion on all levels. That problem is noncommitment. Many people today are unwilling to commit to anything, including God! Without a commitment, there is no direction and no true North by which to orient your life. A commitment is something that doesn't change, but keeps you moving forward in spite of your changing thoughts and feelings. It becomes an act of the will (a decision), empowered by God's Spirit, to keep you on course. As mentioned above, a well-defined purpose gives meaning to life. It is not only your purpose for living but the reason for doing all of the things you do in life. Writing a personal purpose statement sets boundaries in life and enables you to focus clearly.

How much time have you spent reflecting on the purpose of your life?

Have you ever drafted your own personal "purpose statement?" If so, what is it?

A well-written and Christ-centered purpose statement will give you excitement and a renewed focus every time you read or say it. If you have already written one, read through it again. Does it increase your energy level and direct your life focus? If you haven't written one, read on for some key steps to help you draft it. A well-written purpose statement will become your true North that guides your thoughts and actions. As a Christian, a Purpose Statement is not your god, but it should keep you focused on God.

After accepting Christ, knowing your purpose is the most important key to fully living. God the Father, through Jesus Christ, has a purpose and plan for your life. However, He has given you free will. You can choose and desire whatever you want. You decide and commit in your own heart where you want your life to go. God will carry out—or not carry out—His plan for your life based on your willingness to surrender your desires and commitments to His will.

The extent to which God accomplishes His plan for your life is affected by your "will" and is contingent upon your willingness to submit to His purpose for your life. Jesus died in order for us to have free will. He refuses to control us. God honors your will and choices! He will, however, show you His purpose for your life if you choose to commit to Him.

Proverbs 16:9 – "In his heart a man chooses his path but the Lord directs his steps."

Before you begin developing your own purpose statement, it is important to realize that God, through the Holy Spirit, will help you in this process. There is one important example for you to consider before beginning this journey. Let's take a look at the example of Jesus Christ.

If you were to guess the purpose statement of Jesus, what would you say it was?

Christ was sent to this earth to do many things, such as to come so that they may live, come to fulfill the law, come to serve rather than to be served, etc. However, none of these were Christ's purpose statement; they were a result of it. His actual purpose is found in Hebrews 10:7 – "I have come to do your will, Oh God." He based everything he did on that commitment to the Father.

God's plan is your calling, as well as your daily life. Christ had great clarity in following the Holy Spirit because He was sinless in His relationship with the Father. Your purpose should spur you on to do God's will in order to produce in you a full and abundant life.

My own purpose statement took me some time to write. Even when I was done, I felt God had me add some things to it a couple years later. However, every time I quote it (which is every morning) it keeps me focused on following God and his plan.

My personal purpose statement is the following:

"I am a beloved child of God who values loving Him, listening to Him, and following Him always."

Now it's your turn. Before you start this section, get a few blank pieces of paper, a notebook or journal, or even your computer. Use whatever you feel most comfortable with to capture this information and be able to refer to it later.

Steps to Writing Your Personal Purpose Statement:

Step 1 – Set aside time to draft your Purpose Statement:

It's important to set aside some focused time to pray, read the Bible, and think clearly about the answers to the following questions. Most people will need between 1-3 hours to do this. Remember that once you finish it, you may still do some tweaking to it days, weeks, months, or years later. I felt God lead me to add some things to mine nearly 10 years after I drafted it.

Step 2 – Meditate on Scriptures that relate to God's purpose for you:

Think about key aspects from God's Scripture and what He calls us to live by so that we can live the life and receive the promises He has for us. Here are some key Scriptures to consider as you draft your Purpose Statement.

Write down 5-10 key words that stand out to you from reading these Scriptures and determine why they stand out to you. Begin identifying common themes to these words and attributes.

1 Corinthians 13: 4-8, "Love is patient, love is kind. It does not envy, it does not boast, it is not proud. It does not dishonor others, it is not self-seeking, it is not easily angered, it keeps no record of wrongs. Love does not delight in evil but rejoices with the truth. It always protects, always trusts, always hopes, always perseveres. Love never fails."

Galatians 5: 22-23, " But the fruit of the Spirit is love, joy, peace, forbearance, kindness, goodness, faithfulness, gentleness, and self-control. Against such things there is no law."

2 Peter 1:5-11, "For this very reason, make every effort to add to your faith goodness; and to goodness, knowledge; and to knowledge, self-control; and to self-control, perseverance; and to perseverance, godliness; and to godliness, mutual affection; and to mutual affection, love. For if you possess these qualities in increasing measure, they will keep you from being ineffective and unproductive in your knowledge of our Lord Jesus Christ. But whoever does not have them is nearsighted and blind, forgetting that they have been cleansed from their past sins. Therefore, my brothers and sisters, make every effort to confirm your calling and election. For if you do these things, you will never stumble, and you will receive a rich welcome into the eternal kingdom of our Lord and Savior Jesus Christ."

Romans 8:1-39, "Therefore, there is now no condemnation for those who are in Christ Jesus, because through Christ Jesus the law of the Spirit who gives life has set you free from the law of sin and death. For what the law was powerless to do because it was weakened by the flesh, God did by sending his own Son in the likeness of sinful flesh to be a sin offering. And so he condemned sin in the flesh, in order that the righteous requirement of the law might be fully met in us, who do not live according to the flesh but according to the Spirit. Those who live according to the law have their minds set on what the flesh desires; but those who live in accordance with the Spirit have their minds set on what the Spirit desires. The mind governed by the flesh is death, but the mind governed by the Spirit is life and peace. The mind governed by the flesh is hostile to God; it does not submit to God's law, nor can it do so. Those who are in the realm of the flesh cannot please God. You, however, are not in the realm of the flesh but are in the realm of the Spirit if indeed the Spirit of God lives in you. And if anyone does not have the Spirit of Christ, they do not belong to Christ. But if Christ is in you, then even though your body is subject to death because of sin, the Spirit gives life because of righteousness. And if the Spirit of him who raised Jesus from the dead is living in you, he who raised Christ from the dead will also give life to your mortal bodies because of his Spirit who lives in you. Therefore, brothers and sisters, we have an obligation—but it is not to the flesh, to live according to it. For if you live according to the flesh, you will die; but if by the Spirit you put to death the misdeeds of the body, you will live. For those who are led by the Spirit of God are the children of God. The Spirit you received does not make you slaves, so that you live in fear again; rather, the Spirit you received brought about your adoption to sonship. And by him we cry, "*Abba,* Father." The Spirit himself testifies with our spirit that we are God's children. Now if we are children, then we are heirs—heirs of God and co-heirs with Christ, if indeed we share in his sufferings in order that we may also share in his glory. I consider that our present sufferings are not worth comparing with the glory that will be revealed in us. For the creation waits in eager expectation for the children of God to be revealed. For the creation was subjected to frustration, not by its own choice, but by the will of the one who subjected it, in hope that the creation itself will be liberated from its bondage to decay and brought into the freedom and glory of the children of God. We know that the whole creation has been groaning as in the pains of childbirth right up to the present time. Not only so, but we ourselves, who have the first fruits of the Spirit, groan inwardly as we wait eagerly for our adoption to sonship, the redemption of our bodies. For in this hope we were saved. But hope that is seen is no hope at all. Who hopes for what they already have? But if we hope for what we do not yet have, we wait for it patiently. In the same way, the Spirit helps us in our weakness. We do not know what we ought to pray for, but the Spirit himself intercedes for us through wordless groans. And he who searches our hearts knows the mind of the Spirit, because the Spirit intercedes for God's people in accordance with the will of God. And we know that in all things God works for the good of those who love him, who have been called according to his purpose. For those God foreknew he also predestined to be conformed to the image of his Son, that he might be the firstborn among many brothers and sisters. And those he predestined, he also called; those he called, he also justified; those he justified, he also glorified. What, then, shall we say in response to these things? If God is for us, who can be against us? He who did not spare his own Son, but gave him up for us all—how will he not also, along with him, graciously give us all things? Who will bring any charge against those whom God has chosen? It is God who justifies. Who then is the one who condemns? No one. Christ Jesus who died—more than that, who was raised to life—is at the right hand of God and is also interceding for us. Who shall separate us from the love of Christ? Shall trouble or hardship or persecution or famine or nakedness or danger or sword? As it is written: "For your sake we face death all day long; we are considered as sheep to be slaughtered. No, in all these things we are more than conquerors through him who loved us. For I am convinced that neither death nor life, neither angels nor demons, neither the present nor the future, nor any powers, neither height nor depth, nor anything else in all creation, will be able to separate us from the love of God that is in Christ Jesus our Lord."

Proverbs 3:1-35, "My son, do not forget my teaching, but keep my commands in your heart, for they will prolong your life many years and bring you peace and prosperity. Let love and faithfulness never leave you; bind them around your neck, write them on the tablet of your heart. Then you will win favor and a good name in the sight of God and man. Trust in the Lord with all your heart and lean not on your own understanding; in all your ways submit to Him, and he will make your paths straight. Do not be wise in your own eyes; fear the Lord and shun evil. This will bring health to your body and nourishment to your bones. Honor the Lord with your wealth, with the first fruits of all your crops, then your barns will be filled to overflowing, and your vats will brim over with new wine. My son, do not despise the Lord's discipline, and do not resent his rebuke, because the Lord disciplines those he loves, as a father the son he delights in. Blessed are those who find wisdom, those who gain understanding, for she is more profitable than silver and yields better returns than gold. She is more precious than rubies; nothing you desire compares with her. Long life is in her right hand; in her left hand are riches and honor. Her ways are pleasant ways, and all her paths are peace. She is a tree of life to those who take hold of her; those who hold her fast will be blessed. By wisdom the Lord laid the earth's foundations, by understanding he set the heavens in place; by his knowledge the watery depths were divided, and the clouds let drop the dew. My son, do not let wisdom and understanding out of your sight, preserve sound judgment and discretion; they will be life for you, an ornament to grace your neck. Then you will go on your way in safety, and your foot will not stumble. When you lie down, you will not be afraid; when you lie down, your sleep will be sweet. Have no fear of sudden disaster or of the ruin that overtakes the wicked, for the Lord will be at your side and will keep your foot from being snared. Do not withhold good from those to whom it is due, when it is in your power to act. Do not say to your neighbor, "Come back tomorrow and I'll give it to you" when you already have it with you. Do not plot harm against your neighbor, who lives trustfully near you. Do not accuse anyone for no reason-when they have done you no harm. Do not envy the violent or choose any of their ways. For the Lord detests the perverse but takes the upright into his confidence. The Lord's curse in on the house of the wicked, but he blesses the home of the righteous. He mocks proud mockers but shows favor to the humble and oppressed. The wise inherit honor, but fools get only shame.

Step 3 – What is most important to you in life and why?

After reading the Scriptures above, and any others that come to mind, start writing down words describing what is most important to you in life. You might also think about experiences you have had in your faith, an urge God has put on your heart, or other times when you "felt God's pleasure" in what you were doing. These can also help you formulate your Purpose Statement.

Step 4 – Spiritual beliefs and view of eternity:

Write down a few sentences that describe your belief in God and your view of eternity. This is important because you may read and understand God's Word and promises, but if your core beliefs do not line up with them, then you could get off track. It would be a sin to miss the mark of what God has purposed for your life by drafting a purpose statement that is not in the center of His will for you.

It's important to consider your life here on this earth in light of eternity and contemplate what drives your decision-making. For an additional resource on this, I have written *Made to Change the World: Your Life Matters*.

Step 5– Begin to draft your Purpose Statement:

As you think through some of the things you have already written and listed above, it's almost time to start drafting your Powerful Purpose statement that glorifies God and will guide your life. To get started, make two columns on your paper and label the left column "What is most important in my life?" and the right column "Why is that so important to me?"

Step 6–Refining your priority list:

From everything you have done and read above, write down four words or adjectives that would describe the most meaningful life you could live for God. These will most likely be words you will include in your Personal Purpose Statement. If this is difficult, you can start with 8 or 10 then start narrowing it down. Again, this should be done prayerfully.

A way to help you see your top four more clearly it to write each word out on index cards and then lay them out in front of you. Pick the absolute highest priority card first, second, next and so forth until you prioritize your words.

Step 7–First draft of your Purpose Statement:

Read back through the things you listed above. Look for common themes, ideas, and driving factors in your life. Now take a few attempts to draft your own Personal Purpose statement based on those powerful areas described above. Your first draft will most likely be longer than one sentence, so write up to three sentences on your first draft to explain what you want to express.

Step 8–Fine-tuning your Purpose Statement:

Now that you have the first draft of your statement, take the most powerful pieces of what you drafted and condense it all into one sentence. This may start out as a really long sentence. No, despite what you are thinking, you can't create one long run-on sentence. That would be tempting, however! Most likely you will have to remove half or more of what you wrote in your original draft to streamline it. It may not be smooth the first time you get it to one sentence, but that is normal.

Step 9 – Drafting your Purpose Statement:

Does what you drafted for your purpose statement give you: 1) energy and 2) focus when you read it? If so, congratulations! You have drafted your purpose statement. If not, keep working on it and fine-tuning it over days and weeks until it "hits the spot".

Once you have the Purpose Statement the way you want it, memorize it and repeat it each morning. Ideally, you should be able to back it up with Bible Scriptures. You can add Scriptures as references and memorize those as well. One final point is that what you drafted here is not set in stone. Over the months and years to come, you will probably keep refining it.

Step 10–Live it!

You didn't spend all this time, effort, and soul searching to write out your Purpose Statement just to forget about it. I hope you wrote your Purpose Statement so you will have a foundation for committing your life to God based on who He has designed you to be and what He has called you to do.

It can be tempting to start making changes in your own power but it won't last very long. True transformation in life only comes through God's power and the direction of the Holy Spirit. God will lead you and has the ability to open and close every door.

Next, it's time to draft your personal Mission Statement. This will help you spell out what you will *do* as you commit to live your purpose. We are not called to be individual warriors in fulfilling our life's purpose; this will only be fulfilled as we work together with the body of Christ.

It is important to have support as you live your life purpose. That support can come from a spouse, family member, close friend, accountability partner, or pastor. If you would like to take things to the next level through coaching, let me know by e-mailing me at coachbrianwilliams@gmail.com.

DEVELOPING YOUR PERSONAL MISSION STATEMENT

Mission is defined by Webster's New World Dictionary as the following: 1. Ascending out or being sent out to perform a special duty; 2. A group of missionaries (its mission); 3. A diplomatic delegation; 4. A group of technicians, specialists, etc. sent to a foreign country; 5. A special duty for which someone is sent; 6. A special task for which a person is apparently destined in life.

Setting a Personal Mission Statement not only gives you direction for how to fulfill your purpose – it is actually "the way" you will fulfill your purpose. Simply put, a mission statement is a "written focus for your future." It agrees with your purpose for living (you will want to draft your purpose statement before drafting your mission statement if you have not already done so above). An illustration is summarized in this powerful story by Laurie Beth Jones:

"My uncle once told me that during World War II, if an unidentified soldier appeared suddenly in the dark and could not state his mission, he was automatically shot without question." I wonder what would happen if we instituted that policy in today's culture. Most of our generation would be in trouble because we are not trained to think about or live by a mission. One major fear of people living today is not living a life that matters. A well-defined mission gives direction to life.

Now let's look at these together. As a reminder, your Purpose Statement describes your "reason for being" and your Mission Statement is "how to do" your purpose in life.

My Purpose Statement is, *"I am a beloved child of God who values loving Him, listening to Him, and following Him always."*

My Mission Statement is, *"If it be your will, I will live another day and keep myself at my physical, mental, spiritual, and financial peak so I can fulfill my purpose."*

As you can see by "doing" this mission it will help enable me to fulfill my purpose. As you can also see, this is a commitment to God, myself, and others. Notice that it is not detailed to the point that it only focuses on one area of life (such as career, finances, etc.). The specific things you do to fulfill your mission will come later. Just as we see in the example above, the soldier is asked his mission, which might be to take the power supply of the enemy or any number of other possible tasks (missions). The way you actually fulfill your mission can have multiple pathways.

You can start drafting your Mission Statement by reviewing your Personal Purpose Statement again. As you draft your own Mission Statement, it will be an "extension" of your Purpose Statement and will describe what you will do in order to fulfill your purpose in a broad view.

Consider that in a job interview, the interviewer asks what your goals are in life when determining if you are right for the company. If they were to hire you, they would show you all the things you need to know for the job and how to succeed and become prosperous.

However, for them to invest this time and energy into your future, they would want you to commit to them for the long term. They would expect you to follow directions and regulations, come in on time, be ready to work, lead others, and the list goes on. This is the same principle with God: He will reveal in you all of His plans for your life, but

He expects your full, lifelong commitment to Him. You must be committed to God (and His ways), not just to His mission for your life. If you don't have a high enough mission in life, you will stumble through it!

Similarly, imagine if God conducted an interview in which He asked you what you wanted your mission in life to be. In order to place you (His destiny for your life based on your choice), your answer would not only require words, but it would also involve a commitment from you to fulfill it.

As in the previous step, before you begin developing your own Mission Statement, it is important to look to the example of Christ.

As we have learned, Jesus' purpose for coming to this earth was described in Hebrews 10:7— "I have come to do your will, Oh God."

He based everything he did on that commitment. So what was his mission? In Luke 19:10 and John 10:10, we see how and why Jesus surrendered his life on the Cross. We might be able to extrapolate that his Mission Statement was: *"I have come to seek and save the lost so that they may have life and have it to the full."*

Our responsibility, after accepting Christ, is to live as God calls us to live, not only by doing His will but striving to live righteous and holy lifestyles (in mind, body, and spirit) out of love for Him. We are responsible for deciding how we want our thoughts, actions, etc. to glorify God but He will give us strength, wisdom, and guidance if we choose Him with our lives.

Writing your Personal Mission Statement:

Above, you have seen my Personal Mission Statement as well as a plausible snapshot of Jesus' Mission Statement. Here are some examples of corporate mission statements. They are a little different from Personal Mission Statements, but will still get your mind thinking about a well-written mission statement.

1) The Wall Street Journal's Mission Statement is: "To give fully and fairly the daily news attending the fluctuations in prices of stocks, bonds and some commodities."

2) Focus on the Family's Mission Statement is: "To cooperate with the Holy Spirit in disseminating the Gospel of Jesus Christ to as many people as possible…"

3) Lexus' Mission Statement is: "In relentless pursuit of perfection."

Some Christians might wonder if it's important or even Godly to draft your Purpose and Mission Statements. Let's see what God's Word has to say about it. Here are some Scriptures to review and you may come up with some of your own to add to this list.

Proverbs 14:8 - "The wisdom of the prudent is to give thought to their ways, but the folly of fools is deception."

Proverbs 16:2-3 - "All a man's ways seem innocent to him, but motives are weighed by the Lord. Commit to the Lord whatever you do, and your plans will succeed."

Ephesians 5:17 - "Therefore do not be foolish, but understand what the Lord's will is."

Your Mission Statement…

1) Must govern every area of your life (work, ministry, family, relationships, etc.) and agree with your purpose statement.

2) Should be short and to the point (only one sentence long).

3) Should be easily understood by a 12-year-old - "The greater the mission, the more simply it can be stated."

4) Should be in accordance with God's Word, based on your faith & beliefs, in line with your Christian values, stirring up a passion within you, promoting action, and always driving you to progress along God's path.

5) Should be able to be recited instantly.

6) Should be given much prayer and thought.

7) Should only be considered complete when you feel the peace of God in your spirit.

Any time you look at your mission statement, you should be able to say: "I am striving every day to live up to the high standard of this calling. I may not always be successful at it, but I know that as I seek God and follow this call, He will grant me the courage, strength, wisdom, and guidance to complete the task by His power and in His love."

Steps to Writing Your Personal Mission Statement:

Step 1 – Review your Purpose Statement from before and begin to think of 5-10 ideas that come to your mind that would enable you to fulfill that Purpose and write them below.

- Example 1 – Study and memorize God's Word.
- Example 2 – Use my talents to serve others.
- Example 3 – Spend every day in communication with God through prayer
- Example 4 – Use my business to witness to others
- Example 5 - Be a father/mother who reflects Jesus to my kids at all times

Now, write down the ideas that come to your mind.

Step 2 – List one to three things that you are very passionate about in life.

These could be areas of life that you get extremely excited about working on or contributing to, such as helping orphans or developing new areas of service. They could also be areas of life that you are really passionate about changing or improving, such as helping battered women, ending human trafficking, etc.

- Area of passion #1
- Area of passion #2

- Area of Passion #3

Step 3 – Identify the top five talents, gifts, or abilities that seem to come natural to you.

Think about why people are naturally drawn to you. Be specific. It is very common for people to "like" a certain direction in life, but it is not always a good fit for them based on their talents, abilities, and gifting. God wired you to be powerful by operating in the things He has already given you and the abilities yet to be acquired by you.

Step 4 - Pray about how God wants to use you, your talents, your abilities, and your gifts to show your love to Him and to others.

As you pray and wait for Him, write down the things you believe he is showing you through peace in your spirit, Scriptures that come to mind, situations that have happened, or words people have shared with you. Record what God is showing you.

Step 5 – Draft your Personal Mission Statement:

This may take more than one draft to work through fully, and just as with the Purpose Statement above, you may start out with more than one sentence. If you do start out with two or more sentences, keep refining it down to one sentence that is power-packed and hits home for you.

Example:

My Personal Mission is…

Step 6 – Ask yourself some questions to make sure your Mission Statement is fully formed and powerful to you.

If you cannot yet answer "yes" to all of these questions, it will be important for you to keep refining your mission statement until you can.

Is your Mission Statement…

- only one sentence?

- powerful when you read it?
- understandable by a 12-year-old?
- able to be memorized and easily quoted?
- giving you direction?
- glorifying to God?
- helping others?

DEVELOPING YOUR PERSONAL VISION STATEMENT

Why is having vision for your future important? The answer is simple yet extremely profound. It is given to us in Proverbs 29:18, which says, "without vision, the people perish." This truth couldn't be any more powerful because if you do not have an inspiring vision from God for your future, it basically means you are dying.

A powerful story to confirm exactly this point was written by a man named Viktor Frankl in his book, *Man's Search for Meaning*. Victor was a Jewish man who was stuck in a Nazi death camp for several years during the Holocaust. He survived this horrific time in our world and became a therapist to help other people based on what he learned as a prisoner. He found that those who survived the death camps had something in common: they were looking forward to seeing someone or doing something in the future. Basically, they had hope in their hearts and could picture it in their minds. Some of these hopes were based on very small things, but it kept them going. The prisoners who died were the ones who had lost their vision and hope that good things could happen.

What is your vision? Is it powerful and motivating or is it disheartening? Do you even have a vision that God has given you? The key to moving forward in life is to first know your purpose and mission, then to have a BIG vision of what God could bring about as you follow Him.

Keep in mind that when God gives you a vision, most times the end result will not be exactly what you picture in your mind. God may place you on a path that does not resemble what you are expecting. Let's use the example of the captive Israelites before God sent Moses to free them. They were slaves and probably feeling stuck with no future.

Moses comes along, and promises the Israelites that God will not only give them freedom, but also abundance as they flee to a land "flowing with milk and honey." I am sure that every Israelite who heard this promise had a picture in their mind about what that land looked like. The vision in each of their minds of what the land would look like was probably different, but whatever they envisioned, it inspired them and encouraged them to move forward. When they actually saw the Promised Land, it likely didn't look like what any had envisioned, but when they arrived, that didn't matter. What did matter was that God used Moses, the promise, and the vision to inspire His people, which led to freedom.

The second key point is that most of them probably also pictured how easily they would get to their destination. The presumption that it would be a simple journey and easy road was far from reality. It took the Israelites over 40 years and some very harsh trials to finally enter the Promised Land. Keep in mind that nearly all these trials and the long years of wandering in the desert were because of their complaining and lack of faith. Don't let this happen to you as you follow God's plan.

Imagine for a minute that the Israelites did not rebel, and had complete faith as they walked God's path to entering the Promised Land. They still would have been stuck at the Red Sea (until God parted it), they still would have had testing of their patience, and they still would have had to fight the Canaanites to get it. Even when Joshua finally led the nation into the Promised Land, it took seven years to fully conquer the people who were living there and to claim it.

The keys to remember so far is that a vision from God will help inspire you to move forward into huge accomplishments for His name, but most likely, the vision you see will not be the same as the actual result. God's result will always be better. Remember Ephesians 3:20 where it says that glory belongs "to him who is able to do immeasurably more than all we ask or imagine, according to his power that is at work within us."

Secondly, the vision is not just handed to you. You will have to walk by faith, follow diligently, and many times work for it (do your part) for it to come to pass. An important point to remember is that faith is both a noun, which is something you have, and a verb, which is something you do. We have faith but also need to exercise it.

The final point to learn about God's vision and direction is that He will be with you always! We are to keep the "same attitude as that of Christ Jesus" (1 Peter 4:1). When it seems like everything is going wrong and the vision has all but died, keep praising God.

Habakkuk 3:15-20 is a great example of this:

"Though the fig tree does not bud and there are no grapes on the vines, though the olive crop fails and the fields produce no food, though there are no sheep in the pen and no cattle in the stalls, yet I will rejoice in the Lord, I will be joyful in God my Savior."

This is all part of the process! Believe in Him (not the vision itself) and He will do what needs to be done. One last point is that the Israelites who did not believe they could conquer the Canaanites and complained about it never entered the Promised Land. It was the next generation who inherited the land.

Christian Perspective

To really understand the importance of hope and vision, let's take a deeper dive into how it was used in the Bible and what that means for us today. This can help you see how closely hope is tied to vision and how without a powerful vision (or direction) from God, life can feel empty. Below are some excerpts from the *Hayford Bible Handbook* written by Jack Hayford and published by Thomas Nelson Publishers (1995).

Let's start with the word hope or "tiquah" from Scripture. This word means having an "expectation; something yearned for and anticipated eagerly; something for which one waits. Biblical hope rests on God's promises, particularly pertaining to Christ." Hope is never inferior to faith but is an extension of faith. Faith is the present possession of grace; hope is confidence in grace's future accomplishments. Hope is a firm assurance about things that are unseen and still in the future (Rom. 8:24-25, Hebrews 11:7).

As you may recall from earlier, "Now faith is confidence in what we hope for and assurance about what we do not see" Hebrews 11:1. Bill Johnson says, "If it isn't glistening with hope, it isn't God." You can already see how closely faith and hope are tied together. Since faith is the foundation of our belief in Christ and God says that we are sinning when not acting in faith, we must have hope to fuel our faith.

If faith is being sure of what we hope for, then we must know what we hope for! Hope is for the future and is something we look forward to and see in our mind (vision). Hope from God gives us not just an earthly perspective as we live each day, but an eternal view for the future.

The word vision (chazon) also has a powerful meaning. It means, "Prophetic vision, dream, oracle, revelation, especially the kind of revelation that comes through sight, namely a vision from God. In the Bible, people who had visions were filled with a special consciousness of God. Visions never supersede Scripture, but are to be tested by the word (1 Pet. 1:16-21) and judged (1 Corinthians 14:29)- that is, evaluated by a mature believer."

If you look at the biblical meaning of this word, you will see that there is a great importance placed on the priority of Scripture and testing by the Word. Anyone can have a vision! Even Hitler had a vision, but definitely not one from God. Having a vision to hope for and build your faith is important, but only if it is from God. To have a true vision, it must be inspired by God Himself, it must agree with Scripture, and then it should be evaluated by mature believers. When you get that vision from God, write down the Scripture(s) to back it up and get with some other mature believers in the faith to discuss it.

In order to get some perspective on how God uses visions to inspire us to move forward with Him and provide hope for our future, it's important to see how he has done it in the lives of those we see in the Bible. There are many instances of God providing a vision (direction) to His children in both the Old and New Testaments.

Below is the account of just one family and the vision that God gave a father about his future descendants. The vision was not only confirmed by God to this family, but came to pass and still is in place to this day. Take a look into the lives of the following key characters in the Bible and then ask yourself these questions:

How big was the vision God gave this person?

How did this person know to act upon the vision?

What was the impact of trusting and following God's plan based on the vision?

Abraham:

In Genesis 15, we are told that Abraham was promised by God to become the Father of Israel.

Then the word of the LORD came to him: "This man will not be your heir, but a son who is your own flesh and blood will be your heir." He took him outside and said, "Look up at the sky and count the stars—if indeed you can count them." Then he said to him, "So shall your offspring be."

Abram believed the LORD, and he credited it to him as righteousness. God also told Abraham what his descendants would go through in the future in order to become a nation: As the sun was setting, Abram fell into a deep sleep, and a thick and dreadful darkness came over him. Then the LORD said to him, "Know for certain that for four hundred years your descendants will be strangers in a country not their own and that they will be enslaved and mistreated there. But I will punish the nation they serve as slaves, and afterward they will come out with great possessions. You, however, will go to your ancestors in peace and be buried at a good old age. In the fourth generation your descendants will come back here, for the sin of the Amorites has not yet reached its full measure."

Isaac- the promised son of Abraham

God confirmed the vision and promise to Isaac about the nation of Israel. In Genesis, the LORD appeared to Isaac and said,

"Do not go down to Egypt; live in the land where I tell you to live. Stay in this land for a while, and I will be with you and will bless you. For to you and your descendants I will give all these lands and will confirm the oath I swore to your father Abraham. I will make your descendants as numerous as the stars in the sky and will give them all these lands, and through your offspring all nations on earth will be blessed, because Abraham obeyed me and did everything I required of him, keeping my commands, my decrees and my instructions."

Jacob – the son of Isaac

God confirmed the future He had for this family through a dream to Jacob. The account of this story is found in Genesis 28.

He had a dream in which he saw a stairway resting on the earth, with its top reaching to heaven, and the angels of God were ascending and descending on it. There above it stood the LORD, and he said: "I am the LORD, the God of your father Abraham and the God of Isaac. I will give you and your descendants the land on which you are lying. Your descendants will be like the dust of the earth, and you will spread out to the west and to the east, to the north and to the south. All peoples on earth will be blessed through you and your offspring. I am with you and will watch over you wherever you go, and I will bring you back to this land. I will not leave you until I have done what I have promised you."

Joseph – the son of Jacob

When Joseph received a vision from God through a dream (a vision received while asleep) he told his brothers and was nearly murdered because of it. However, the very thing that almost got him killed was what God used to raise him up at a later time. In Genesis 37, Joseph had a dream, and when he told it to his brothers, they hated him all the more. He said to them,

"Listen to this dream I had: We were binding sheaves of grain out in the field when suddenly my sheaf rose and stood upright, while your sheaves gathered around mine and bowed down to it." His brothers said to him, "Do you intend to reign over us? Will you actually rule us?" And they hated him all the more because of his dream and what he had said. Then he had another dream, and he told it to his brothers. "Listen," he said, "I had another dream, and this time the sun and moon and eleven stars were bowing down to me." When he told his father as well as his brothers, his father rebuked him and said, "What is this dream you had? Will your mother and I and your brothers actually come and bow down to the ground before you?" His brothers were jealous of him, but his father kept the matter in mind.

In each of the Biblical accounts above, the characters received a vision from God. However, like ours, their visions did not always come to fruition how they had pictured, but their faith in God drove them to persevere. In the end, God's plan and purpose prevailed. He was and is always true and faithful to His word.

This is every bit as true today as it was then. Your vision from God may not always seem possible by your limited human understanding, and sometimes it can feel like the vision has died. But if it is from God, you can stand as strongly as those in times of old upon His truth and promises. You alone cannot bring a vision to pass for you or anyone else; only God can. However, you are expected to believe that He can and will bring to pass what He promises. Once you have a vision from God, it will also have you! You will know it is what God has made you to do when it excites you each time you think about it.

As I have given you my personal Purpose and Mission statement above, I will also give you my Vision Statement which is, *"All who have accepted Christ, including me, would fulfill their purpose and mission, and those who have not accepted Him would come to accept Him."*

This is the vision that drives me to help Christians, including myself, to become all that God has in store for them, and to make it a priority to witness to anyone who is not yet in God's family.

What would you guess Jesus' vision would have been while He walked the face of the earth? Although He doesn't specifically give us His vision statement, we can take a good guess at it from Scripture. What did you come up with? If I were to guess, one Scripture immediately comes to mind, is 2 Peter 3:9 – "not willing that any should perish, but that all should come to repentance." That is definitely a big vision that refers to the whole world and everyone that has come and gone since the birth of Christ.

DREAMS, VISIONS, AND GOALS

When your desires, emotions (passion), and logic are in one accord and can support your specific vision (assuming your vision lines up biblically with God's Word and can be pursued by faith), embrace it and believe in the vision God gave you. Remember, you can only accomplish your calling with God's power through Christ's blood and the guidance of the Holy Spirit. It is therefore critically important to understand the Lord's will concerning your vision by knowing if and when you are to pursue them.

The following, in addition to much prayer, is a way to help establish, understand, and realize your dreams for life.

Vision from God not only fulfills you, but also glorifies Him. God will give you dreams to accomplish His plans and fulfill your life. Pray for big dreams from God but know that conceited, selfish dreams are too small for Him. Eliminate them from your life! Choose to see what God wants to show you and expect big things!

One caution here is that as you get vision and direction from God, many times His time frame will be much different from yours. I can think of many times where I felt God gave me a direction and vision and off I went, only to realize I was by myself trying to make it happen and getting nowhere. As you can see from the Scriptures above and how God worked through the family of Israel, it took quite a while and there were many obstacles to overcome. Abraham's son Ishmael is a good example of this. Sarah grew impatient to have a son and urged her husband Abraham to sleep with her servant. Ishmael became the result of that union and because of that choice to take things into their own hands, the descendants of Ishmael are still enemies of Israel (descendants of Abraham and Sarah) today.

"If you'll not settle for anything less than your best, you will be amazed at what you can accomplish in your lives." – Vince Lombardi.

Do the things that God wants you to be doing—no more and no less.

Here are some steps to draft your God-given vision. It is important to make sure your vision is biblical and from God, so working through these steps will help you.

Steps to Writing Your Personal Vision Statement:

Step 1 –Review your Purpose and Mission Statements

If you have already completed the sections above related to developing your Purpose and Mission Statement, a lot of key work has already been completed. These are important components to review and keep in focus as you draft your vision so that your vision lines up with your purpose and what you are called to do.

Step 2–Brainstorm and write all the ideas that come to mind for your vision.

Don't worry about format or being wordy; just get your thoughts down on paper. As you do this, pray that God will reveal His vision for your life to you. This is an exciting process, so make the most of your time doing this.

Many times, it is helpful to write these ideas down for each area of your life. Although you may have several areas of your life that you want or need to improve, you can really only focus on one at a time. This exercise will help you write out your ideas concerning your vision for each area of your life; try to write at least three adjectives, words, Scriptures, or phrases for each area.

Spiritual:

Mental:

Physical:

Family:

Relationships:

Career:

Finances:

Recreation:

Step 3–Narrow your vision down to one sentence

This next step can be challenging. You probably have many ideas already drafted from the step above and consider them all important. However, for this to become powerful for you, easily remembered, and able to keep you focused, you will want to choose one area and narrow it down to one sentence. You may need to start with several sentences to begin with and then start pulling out words (keeping the key words in) to pare it down to one sentence.

It may take several days, or even several weeks to finish this process, but continue to write and pray about this for as long as needed. You can also run your thoughts by close friends, family, pastors, or your life-coach. It may help to refer to some of the examples above as you continue over time to refine your words that will aptly express your vision. It does not have to be perfect; it just needs to capture the essence of your direction.

Step 4–Read over your vision

After you have finished with drafting your vision, set it aside for some time. This could be hours or even days. The idea is to take your mind off of it so you can come back to it with fresh eyes. When you do pick it up again, read it and see how you feel about it.

Does it give you hope and excitement? Do you feel peace in your heart that this is from God?

If you feel that what you have written is a good fit, then keep it just the way it is. If something still seems off, make the adjustments as needed.

Step 5–Surrender it to God

Even though you have spent time drafting your Purpose, Mission, and Vision Statements and have sought God through the process, the ultimate direction and plan for your life is in His hands. Surrender these things to Him. Ask Him to show you what, if anything, needs to be changed in your focus for living. Let Him know that your commitment is not to "doing" things, but to "being" who he has called you to be by loving Him and loving others.

Step 6–Review and quote your vision daily

Those things on which you have spent your time, effort and energy could seem like just a trivial "homework assignment," or it can be life-changing. If you put it out of sight and out of mind, it will just be something that you review once every year or two, like old letters or cards from others. However, if you start reviewing, or better yet, memorizing your powerful life statements, they will keep you focused on God and His plan for your life.

The first thing I do in the morning is quote the powerful promises in Scripture as God leads. I have memorized at least 30 verses, including some full chapters, and I have internalized them. Every day, I start out quoting them and then quote my Purpose, Mission, and Vision statements.

The work you have done is no small thing. It will culminate into something powerful. Next, you will begin to put a plan of action in place to live it all out.

PLAN OF ACTION: HOW TO LIVE YOUR PURPOSE, MISSION, AND VISION

Congratulations! You have done more already than most people do in their lifetime by taking time to think about and write your Purpose, Mission, and Vision Statements. These should summarize God's direction in your life and what your commitments should be. Now, let's talk about how to put them into practice.

Imagine that the best architect in the word drafted the most spectacular building ever designed, but he never told anyone about it and never moved forward with plans to build it. That would be a waste of talent! God did not give you talent to waste, but to use in impactful ways for His kingdom. God won't make you do anything, but He will use you as you are willing to walk forward in his plan. There is a great quote that says, "God can't steer a sitting ship." Are you willing to be moved by God?

Many Christians have asked me if our walk and circumstances are in our control and our responsibility or if God just makes things happen as He sees fit. The answer is "yes" to both. Proverbs 19:21 says, "Many are the plans in a person's heart, but it is the LORD's purpose that prevails."

There are many places in the Bible that talk about us making plans. The most important part is to ask God to show you the direction He would have you take. Even as you plan your course and walk that path, always let God change, move, or adjust it as He wishes. God can steer you along the right path when you are moving, but if you are just sitting around and expecting Him to do everything, you will miss out. Passivity will rob you of the journey He intends for you.

Even Jesus moved and walked with God. Sure, he spent lots of time in prayer talking with his Father, but then he would go into the world and let his Father work through him. Think about it this way: the Great Commandment (*Love* the Lord your God with all your heart, mind and strength) and The Great Commission (*Go* into the world and make disciples) are action items, not study materials.

Let's work on some ways to plan your course in order to fulfill your Purpose and Mission and to pursue your Vision. It should not be enough for you to just write them on paper; they should inspire you to take action and see them come to pass. Keep in mind, especially when it comes to vision: if it's from God, it will happen in God's timing, not yours, and you probably will incur some rough water, challenges, and storms along the voyage.

Steps to Create Your Plan of Action:

Step 1 –List all the different goals you have in mind.

When you think about all you would like to achieve in life, there may be only a couple of goals you can list, or there may be many. The first step is to list them all out so they are visible and not just stuck in your mind. Even though your list may be long, you can really only work on one (or at most two) things at a time, so you will need to prioritize. We will walk through a step by step process to help you select the prioritized goals first. Always keep your list handy because even if something is not a priority now, it may become one after you accomplish your other goals.

Step 2–Answer the "why" question.

Next to each goal, answer: "Why is this goal important?" Consider this question from a couple of different perspectives. The first is to understand why God would want you to pursue and attain this goal. Did God show you through Scripture or prayer that he wants you to pursue this goal? If so, move forward. If not, perhaps it is not something God wants for you at this time—and perhaps not at all.

Also, answer the question as to why the goal is important to you. It may be something that you don't have the desire, skills, or calling for. Maybe you are trying to make it one of your goals because someone else thinks it's important or you feel it's a noble cause? Consider whether or not it is the right thing for you to do.

A great quote from Steven Covey says, "Many people climb the ladder of success only to get to the top and find that their ladder is against the wrong wall." This is the step where you can prevent climbing wrong ladders because you are taking time to pray and thinking through where to climb.

Step 3–What type of goal are you setting?

When setting goals, it's important to remember two key factors. First, there are different types of goals. Some goals lead to habit change (such as wanting to exercise three days per week or to start having daily devotions). Other goals have a targeted beginning and end date (such as wanting to join a ministry at church within the next two months). Both are important and both have their place. Start off by looking at your top goal and determining if it is a habit goal or a target goal.

If your goal is to change a habit, once you establish that new habit, you can start working on other goals and areas while checking in to make sure your habit goal is still on track.

Additionally, many times you will find that once a habit is in place, the next step is to adjust or fine-tune. Using one of the examples above, if you now have a daily devotion time of praying and reading the Bible, your next focus may be that you want to add journaling to your devotion time.

If it's a targeted goal you are starting with, then at the end of that time frame or once the goal is accomplished, you will need to look at it to see if it is something you want to continue developing, or if you want to shift your focus to a new goal.

Again, using the example above, if you have become active in ministry, you might want to move on to your next important targeted goal. Or you may also decide to set another goal in this same area (such as dedicating three hours per week to working in your new ministry).

Some important keys to remember in this step are to pray as you move forward on your goals, write them down on paper and keep them in front of you, share them with others who are supportive of you, and continue to let God guide your steps. Also very helpful in this stage is identifying a Scripture or two to support the goal you are pursuing.

Step 4–What is the time frame for your goal?

Just as there are different types of goals, there are different time frames for goals as well. Long-term goals generally take six months to a year to reach. Medium-range goals can run from three to six months and short-term goals, which help you achieve your medium and long-term goals, generally range from days up to a few months.

It is important to set these time frames and targets in order to be successful! You may not always hit them perfectly, but they will give you a tangible target. Even if you underestimate the time needed to accomplish the goal, you will be much further ahead by setting that deadline than by not setting one at all.

Make sure to consider your deadline (be realistic with your time, energy, and learning curve), write it down, and share it with your support network.

Step 5–Break the goal down into smaller steps

You may need to break down those mid- and long-term goals into smaller, more achievable goals along the way in order to stay on pace. For instance, if you set a goal to go on a mission trip in May, many other goals will go into the planning and process to get you there. You will need to think through everything that is involved in going on the mission trip: finances, time, groups, supplies, etc. List as many details as possible to help you prepare and stay on track. Remember the adage, "When people fail to plan, they plan to fail."

Step 6–Draft out your plan.

Once you have a goal and know your direction, you need a plan for accomplishing it. Using a biblical example, King Solomon, the wisest and richest King to have ever taken the throne of Israel, was directed by God to build the Holy Temple. That is one big and exciting goal! However, God knew exactly what he wanted built. He didn't just tell Solomon to go build a temple, leaving it up to Solomon and expecting that it to be exactly what He wanted.

God gave meticulous plans for the temple. He told Solomon how he wanted it to look, how big it would be, and where it would be placed. He also gave key details on the people and skills needed to put it together, materials to be used, and a time frame for completion. God not only gave Solomon the goal, but He also filled in the details. He will do that for you, too!

Take some time now to write out your plan. Describe exactly how you will attain your goal. It should be as detailed as you can make it and should include the following:

- When will you start on this goal?
- What do you need to get started?
- What is the first step that needs to be accomplished?
- Where will you work on this goal (physical space)?
- What do you need to get started (materials)?
- How much money (if any) do you need?

As you may have noticed, many of the questions above focus on getting started and creating momentum. If you want to list all the steps necessary through the process, that is great. However, the first key to success is getting started. Remember, a sitting ship is difficult to move. But momentum fuels itself, so as you start progressing, you will be

PLAN OF ACTION: HOW TO LIVE YOUR PURPOSE, MIS... 51

propelled to take the next steps. Recognize that often, next steps don't become clear until the first steps are accomplished. The water didn't part for Moses until he stepped into it. Then, his next steps became obvious.

Once you have all these things written down, review them with someone you trust. This could be a close Christian friend or family member, a mentor, or your life coach. Walk through the steps and let the person ask you questions. A good test for how well you have written your plan of action is to see if s/he can take your instructions and actually follow them. Your supportive friend's level of understanding will prove to you that you have what you need: a plan with good ideas that is understandable and simplified enough that they could pick up what you have written, follow it, and accomplish it themselves.

Step 7–Get Started!

Once you have narrowed down your focus to your goal (or at most two goals), you have to start working on it or it will just sit on paper and never come to pass. Getting started can be challenging, especially if you have a big goal in front of you. It can also make your face your fears of the unknown or bring up times where you have felt failure in reaching previous goals. However, the final word about this comes from God. If you are seeking God and your vision, goals, and direction are guided by Him, then you can stand on His promises, such as:

Philippians 4:13 – "I can do all thing through him who gives me strength."

Ephesians 3:20 – God "is able to do immeasurably more than all we ask or imagine, according to his power that is at work within us…"

The most important thing to remember as you get started is **"Just start!"** Don't let perfection keep you from taking an action step. Once you are moving forward, you will quickly learn new things and make key adjustments. Don't let the fear of failure hold you back. At the same time, don't be daunted by the fear of success. Walk by faith and do your best with what God has called you to do. Do something—

anything—just to get started and gain momentum. Small changes make a big difference!

Step 8–Plan your time.

Congratulations on the steps you have taken so far to list your goals, draft your plan, and take the first step toward accomplishment. That is huge! God will bless you for your walk of faith.

You have probably found it exciting thinking about what will help you move forward in life. It's also natural to map out your goal and plans, although it does require some thinking. Even taking the first step is usually fun, so most of these steps hopefully were not too difficult for you.

For the majority of people, the challenge begins with efforts to stay on track and continue to work on the goal until it is accomplished. This requires dedication of both time and energy.

It could be that you only need one block of time to accomplish the goal. Other goals may require dedicated daily time blocks. As an example, if your first goal is to turn a room in your house into an office, you might only need one weekend to paint and go buy some furniture. If you have longer-term or habit goals, you will need to schedule accordingly. For example, as I wrote this book, I spent a minimum of 30 minutes per day writing just after my devotions each morning, usually around 6 am.

If you don't have a planning system, this is the perfect time for you to establish one. Many online tools and apps exist for this purpose. The Zig Ziglar *Performance Planner* has been an effective tool for keeping me on track for years. Michael Hyatt's *Full Focus Planner* is another great resource. Planning your time is essential for helping you accomplish your goals, so use whichever tool fits best for you.

Step 9–Find support.

We are all designed by God to work together on this earth. That is why we each have different talents, abilities, likes, and dislikes. We are a family, and in God's family we are to love and support each other.

When you pursue God's plan for your life, He does not desire you to be a lone crusader. If you go that route as you work on your goals, you will not be nearly as successful or impactful as you will be in working together with others. This doesn't mean your support network is taking on all or even any of the tasks for you (although they may be). It does mean that you have someone to provide objective thoughts and opinions.

Solid support means someone is there for you. This person will encourage you through the tough challenges of moving forward, celebrate with you through the successes, and always stand with you as you work to achieve God's plan for your life. It means that you have an ally, a prayer partner, and someone who seeks God on your behalf. At the same time, that person (or group of people) should love you enough to say the hard things to help you grow. Such truth-telling does not mean the person is being negative or pulling you down; telling someone hard but helpful things comes from love and Holy Spirit-led intention.

Great places to find support are: Christian friends/family members, small groups, mentors or pastors, and of course Christian life coaches. A word of caution: be aware that someone close to you may find it harder to be objective.

The job of a life coach is to partner with you—to stand for you and with you to achieve your goals, to challenge you to think bigger and aim higher, and to help you accomplish all God has for you. If you would like to contact me and learn more about life coaching, e-mail: coachbrianwilliams@gmail.com.

LIVE THE ADVENTURE

John Eldridge is a special author whose books and study materials I enjoy reading. For men, he has a book *Wild at Heart* that explains the core of a man as described by God in the Bible. He and his wife also co-wrote *Captivating* which explains the essence of a woman as she was designed by God. Clearly, males and females are different. They often have differing views, priorities, and needs. However, the one thing both have in common is the desire to live an adventurous life.

This desire for adventure may have been stifled at times in your life, but I'm betting that longing for excitement is still there. Why is that? One reason is that God designed us to walk by faith, not by sight. If you are truly living the Christian life and walking by faith, it will inevitably be an adventure! When God asks you to take a step of faith outside your comfort zone, your heart may start pounding, your adrenalin might race, and your mind may go full-throttle.

God wired us to walk with Him, and by doing so, we will be in for an adventure. Don't let the cares and worries of this world choke that out of you. One of my favorite Scriptures is Joshua 1:9, "Have I not commanded you? Be strong and courageous. Do not be afraid; do not be discouraged, for the LORD your God will be with you wherever you go."

God doesn't just ask or recommend that we not worry—He **commands** us not to worry. It is sin if we do something outside of His command.

You have a purpose and reason for being here on this earth today and every day until Christ calls you home to be with Him. You have an exciting mission to fulfill, and God has given you dreams and visions for how to accomplish it.

Now it's time to take your first step toward your goal, so offer it up to God, and then do it! Even if later on you find that you are completely off track, that's okay! God will honor anything done in faith, so if you are faithfully taking steps forward—even with the occasional misstep—God will make your path straight (Proverbs 3:5-6). Live the adventure – it starts today! It is my hope that in doing so, at the end of each day (and at the end of your life), you will hear God say, "Well done, good and faithful servant" (Matthew 25:21).

As always, I would love to hear how all of this is going for you. You can always reach out to me through the "Contact" page of madetochangetheworld.com or e-mail me directly at coachbrianwilliams@gmail.com . If you would also like additional support as you walk God's path for success, you can check out more resources at madetochangetheworld.com. God bless you as you faithfully walk with Him!

Made in the USA
Middletown, DE
06 November 2023

42093860R00040